Endorsements

Has communion become routine, stale, or repetitive? This book is absolutely what you need to break into a fresh place in the Lord through communion. In their book COMMUNION – Activating the Power of God in Everyday Living, Joe and Sandy Sims have captured the heart of God and His many facets of the rich power of the body and blood of Jesus. You'll be made blessed by every single devotion. Joe and Sandy have walked in a love for communion and it's richness over the 26 years we've known them. Let this book deepen your walk with our beloved savior and King.

Dvain and Joel Wolfe

New Horizon Church. Fife. WA

Wow! What an incredible twelve-week devotional!

COMMUNION ... The act of sharing or exchanging intimate thoughts or feelings. Joe and Sandy Sims capture God's invitation to commune. Not just during a special Sunday service led by a certain recited passage of scripture. But, in every day, in every moment, for every area of our life. The following pages are packed with gentle reminders offered throughout Scripture, of God's great desire to commune with you. The fresh insights provided in this devotional will forever change how you think about this special sacrament.

Greg and Julie Gorman

Married for a Purpose Founders

COMMUNION

Activating the Power of God in
Everyday Living

Joe and Sandy Sims

Foreword by Terry Nance
Author of **God's Armorbearer**

Publisher: Married for a Purpose
Hobe Sound, Florida 33455 USA
marriedforapurpose.com

ISBN 9781737917243

Table of Contents -

Foreword
A Note to the Reader
The Salvation Message of Communion

Testimony of Healing

*This book is dedicated to the New Horizon
Church Communion Group.
Thank you for your partnership, patience,
encouragement, and most of all prayer.
We love each one of you!
Joe and Sandy*

*Special thanks to Julie Gorman
And Rina Solano-Castillo.
Without them, this book would have taken
years longer to write and publish.*

This communion journey began when dear friends, Jeff and Karen Conley, were stranded on the Princess cruise ship off the coast of California in March of 2020. During that time, we began daily phone calls to take communion with them while the ship waited for clearance from the government to dock.

Within a short time frame the world became a different place. When churches, businesses and nearly every other necessary place closed, we sensed an urgency to continue meeting daily with our church family for communion.

In response to that sensing we launched a nightly communion group via Zoom. When our regular services resumed on Pentecost Sunday, we shifted to meeting weekly. As of this writing we have met nearly 200 times to take communion.

During our calls we have taken communion, studied the Bible, prayed together, worshiped, supported each other through various difficulties and celebrated life's wins.

Jesus said to take communion in remembrance of Him and to do it often.

We pray this devotional will bless you. We also trust that it will break religious tradition from your life and the power of God will be released as you receive communion!

Foreword -

It has been a joy for myself and my wife Kim to connect with Joe and Sandy Sims over the past few years. They have truly demonstrated a genuine love for Jesus and a desire to lead people into a closer relationship with Him.

It was a wonderful blessing to sit with them recently to hear the revelation God has poured into their hearts on receiving communion from the Lord's table. As they shared with us scriptures in the Old and New Testament, clearly revealing the communion revelation, it was a heart stirring time we had together. Seeing from the Bible how much Jesus has done for us and has shown His love toward us, makes your heart burn within you.

As I read through this book it stirred in me and Kim the desire to make communion a major part of our prayer time. Communion, I believe, is the most sacred institution that a Christian can participate in. We are invited by Jesus to receive communion with Him at any time we desire.

1 Corinthians 11: 24, 25 in the Passion Translation reads:

24. Then he distributed it to the disciples and said, "Take it and eat your fill. It is my body, which is given for you. Do this to remember me.

25. He did the same with the cup of wine after supper and said, "This cup seals the new covenant with my blood. Drink it—and whenever you drink this, do it to remember me."

When we take communion, we are remembering Jesus' sacrifice on the cross. The bread and wine are tangible, visible reminders of Christ's love. Rather than simply saying "remember," Jesus gave us a tangible reminder. Just as we depend on food and drink to live physically, we can only live spiritually through Christ.

Communion is a time of just that: communing. It is a chance to bring ourselves before the Lord and partake in the life He has given us through His death and resurrection.

Jesus called Himself "the bread of life" in Matthew 6:11. It means that we're nourished by Him, we survive because of Him, and He satisfies us when everything else leaves us empty.

There's a connection between our nearness to Jesus, believing in Him and being fulfilled by Him.

The early Church celebrated Jesus by taking communion, sometimes every day. They saw that every time they gathered around a table to eat and drink, it was a chance to recognize Jesus and thank God for all He's done.

Joe and Sandy Sims have shown us through communion, we can reconnect and secure our love for Jesus by daily receiving from the Lord's table. This is something that can be done with a body of believers or done in private in your prayer time.

The words "whenever you drink this" open to us an eternal invitation. Sitting in the presence of Jesus by myself or with my Christian brothers and sisters takes my mind and spirit back to the place of the Cross and the Resurrection. As we receive communion together the spirit of love and unity is burned in our hearts. As I receive communion in my prayer time, I am acknowledging my love for him and all he sacrificed for me.

These daily devotions on communion will stir your heart and thrill your soul as you see the power of God working in you, your family and your life. I believe this book will challenge your heart to make the receiving of communion a priority in your life.

1 Corinthians 11: 26 For as often as ye eat this bread, and drink this cup, you will declare the Lord's death till he come. I pray that today you will allow the Holy Spirit to open your heart through the power of communion. This book will move your life toward a new encounter with Jesus.

Terry Nance
Pastor and Author of God's Armorbearer

A Note to the Reader -

As a child growing up in church I sat through many dozens of communion "services." Looking back, it feels like they were all identical. The pastor's voice seemed to deepen at the mention of this beautiful tradition. Shiny trays full of tiny, stale crackers and tiny cups of juice were passed down each row. If you were visiting or too young to read, you were expected to not take a cracker or juice. The same few Bible verses were read every time and I wasn't very old by the time I had them memorized.

When the minister finished reading, everyone silently bowed their heads, except me. After finally being allowed to consume my mini snack, my mom would give me a stink eye as I tried to lick the last drop of juice from the tiny plastic cup.

I understood this was important but didn't fully understand why. It was very repetitious but not very personal. Even as a child, I had a feeling there was more to this beautiful, mysterious, time-honored tradition.

Maybe you can relate to my story or maybe you're not sure what I'm talking about or maybe you're the pastor I'm talking about. Whichever is the case, I invite you to open your heart and mind to the scriptures and stories in these pages and let them come alive to you.

The more Joe and I study what the Bible has to say on this subject, the greater our realization that we had a few misconceptions and we will never understand it all.

We have learned you don't have to be an ordained minister with special stale crackers to share communion. In fact, you don't have to use a cracker at all.

Communion can be taken at home, from your car, in a hotel or anywhere else you happen to be. You can also take it as often as you want or need to.

We have discovered communion is personal enough to celebrate alone and special enough to celebrate with everyone you can.

As you study these pages, I invite you to use them as they are written, add your own examples and insights or break them into smaller lessons for your children. Use them weekly, monthly or on repeat.

Let them spark your own deep dives into the treasure that is communion!

~ Sandy

The Salvation Message of Communion

If you have never heard of communion or you have heard of it but couldn't really say what it's about, stick with me for a few paragraphs.

Salvation

The foundation of Christianity is the reality of communion. It means a common union or sharing and participating in the same thing. It is this common union that is the very heart of our salvation.

Without salvation we cannot celebrate, remember or truly partake of the cup and bread of communion.

In the prayer Jesus prayed in John 17:20-23, it was this common union that He was desiring for every believer.

"And I ask not only for these disciples, but also for all those who will one day believe in me through their message.
I pray for them all to be joined together as one

even as you and I, Father, are joined together as one. I pray for them to become one with us so that the world will recognize that you sent me.

For the very glory you have given to me I have given them so that they will be joined together as one and experience the same unity that we enjoy.

You live fully in me and now I live fully in them so that they will experience perfect unity, and the world will be convinced that you have sent me, for they will see that you love each one of them with the same passionate love that you have for me." TPT

The unity He was praying for is not just a mere quality of life but it is that our unity in Him would become the center of our lives. In other words, He desires that our relationship with Him would be the nucleus everything from, for and through our lives would flow.

John said it this way in I John 1:5-7

"This is the life-giving message we heard him share and it's still ringing in our ears. We now repeat his words to you: God is pure light. You will never find even a trace of darkness in him.

If we claim that we share life with him, but keep walking in the realm of darkness, we're fooling ourselves and not living the truth.

But if we keep living in the pure light that surrounds him, we share unbroken fellowship with one another, and the blood of Jesus, his Son, continually cleanses us from all sin." TPT

In this passage, our communion with God is described as living in pure light. In other words, living in communion with Him is joining with Him in the pure light that He offers. If we are living in this pure light, then the darkness of sin will be revealed to us. Not to condemn us but to conform us to His image so that we will be in unity with Him.

We must remember that God is love and it is His nature to lovingly correct us as His children, not beat us with conviction. In the same way, if our biological parents corrected us in love that correction probably had better results than the abusive correction some children may have received.

John goes on to say this in verses 8-10:

"If we boast that we have no sin, we're only fooling ourselves and are strangers to the truth.

But if we freely admit our sins when his light uncovers them, he will be faithful to forgive us every time.

God is just to forgive us our sins because of Christ, and he will continue to cleanse us from all unrighteousness. If we claim that we're not guilty of sin when God uncovers it with his light, we make him a liar and his word is not in us."
TPT

Before you receive communion, we want to give you the opportunity to make Jesus Lord of your life.

Prayer

If you have not ever asked Jesus for forgiveness and invited Him to be the Lord of your life or if you once knew Him but have fallen away from your relationship with Him, **we want to invite you to pray this prayer:**

Father God, I thank you for sending Jesus to die on the cross for my sin. I acknowledge my need for His saving power and cleansing.

I ask you to forgive me of my sin and come live in my heart. As this scripture says, I ask to become one with you and that your pure light would fill me.

Thank you for your love and peace that fill me and for the unity I have with you.

If you prayed the salvation prayer we just spoke of, we believe you are now born again. We want to welcome you to the family of God!

Communion

Receiving communion is a central part of our faith. It is both a celebration of what Jesus did for us and a solemn reminder of the price He paid for our redemption.

In John 6:53-58 Jesus describes communion this way:

"Jesus replied to them, "Listen to this eternal truth: Unless you eat the body of the Son of Man and drink his blood, you will not have eternal life.

Eternal life comes to the one who eats my body and drinks my blood, and I will raise him up in the last day.

For my body is real food for your spirit and my blood is real drink.

The one who eats my body and drinks my blood lives in me and I live in him.

The Father of life sent me, and he is my life. In the same way, the one who feeds upon me, I will become his life.

I am not like the bread your ancestors ate and later died. I am the living Bread that comes from heaven. Eat this Bread and you will live forever!" TPT

When we use the phrase "receive communion" or "take communion" we are talking about the practice of eating a wafer, cracker, or bread as a symbol of Jesus' body and taking a drink of juice as a symbol of Jesus' blood. We don't believe that it literally becomes flesh and blood as we eat and drink it.

If you don't have any of these items, use whatever you have available. The most important aspect is your heart honoring what Jesus has done for you. For a more in-depth explanation, read lesson number one, A Form of Godliness.

As you receive Communion pray this prayer: Jesus, as I receive the bread, I partake of the unity that you spoke of in the scriptures. I thank you for your broken body. Thank you that by the stripes you suffered I am healed.

As I receive the cup, I thank you for the blood you shed for me and that by your blood I am forgiven of my sins and purified in you. I receive the freedom you provided for me on the cross.

One

Communion - A Form of Godliness

Have you ever watched a movie, listened to a song, heard a sermon or a speech and not thought much of it? Maybe you even considered it a waste of time while everyone around you thought it was fabulous.

Experience

Even in church, when you love Jesus, worshiping with other believers can be profoundly impactful or it can just be a "song service." As a young teen, I remember looking forward to the monthly song service more for the entertainment value than for the power of God to fall or to truly honor Him.

As I matured, I began to understand the importance and value of sincerely worshiping God. When His anointing came, it was no longer entertainment; it transformed into a love affair. When we experience God's presence, we no longer want to do things religiously. We worship Him expecting a powerful experience.

When it comes to communion, or anything we do regularly, it can be done without expectation or focus. You can participate in the activity but not acknowledge its power. If you grew up in church, you might have taken communion regularly but never understood or experienced the power God intended for you in the bread and cup.

By only going through the motions of communion we can lose the awareness of its authority.

2 Timothy 3:1-5 puts it in perspective: "But *know this, that in the last days perilous times will come:*

For men will be lovers of themselves, lovers of money, boasters, proud, blasphemers, disobedient to parents, unthankful, unholy, unloving, unforgiving, slanderers, without self-control, brutal, despisers of good, traitors, headstrong, haughty, lovers of pleasure rather than lovers of God, having a form of godliness but denying its power. And from such people turn away!" NKJV

Form vs. Power

You can have a form (religion or religious experience that seems godly) but deny its power.

For things to work correctly, we need a form for things to flow through. Electricity needs wiring to flow through. Wire provides the conduit or form. Wire by itself is powerless.

Without a conduit, electricity is useless but with one we connect to electric power. As you take communion by faith you are connecting heaven's supply with your earthly need.

Our obedience to honor and receive the bread and the cup of communion provides the form or conduit. The blood of Jesus and Holy Spirit's anointing on what we are doing provides the power.

Jesus said, eat this bread and drink this cup and you will know the power of covenant.

I Corinthians 11:23-26 states:

"The same night in which He was handed over, He took bread and gave thanks. Then He distributed it to the disciples and said, "Take it and eat your fill.

It is my body, which is given for you. Do this to remember me."

He did the same with the cup of wine after supper and said, "This cup seals the new covenant with my blood. Drink it - and whenever you drink this, do it to remember me."

Whenever you eat this bread and drink this cup, you are retelling the story, proclaiming our Lord's death until He comes." TPT

Every time we take communion, we proclaim the power of Jesus' death and His resurrection. We declare the anointing that was on Him. This bread and cup demonstrate His power and anointing.

He Prepares a Table of Anointing for You

Psalms 23:5 and 6 read, "*You prepare a table before me in the presence of my enemies; You anoint my head with oil; My cup runs over.*

Surely goodness and mercy shall follow me All the days of my life; And I will dwell in the house of the LORD forever." NKJV

He prepares a table in the presence of our enemy. Another way to put it is that He will demonstrate His power right in front of your enemy.

The Bible says in Luke 22 verse 3 that when Jesus and the disciples sat around a table for the last supper, Satan had already entered Judas. Their enemy, Satan, was at the table with them. It was there Jesus took the bread and gave thanks. He then blessed the bread, broke it, and gave it to his disciples saying, "Take and eat for this is my body."

The Father prepared a table for Jesus in the presence of Satan, His enemy! In that environment God showed up and demonstrated His anointing.

The form of communion contains the power of God for our lives. When we receive communion, we consume God's anointing. You may be sitting with an enemy at your table. It could be sickness, confusion, condemnation, depression or anything else that is not God's plan for you. Ultimately God prepares your table. At the table prepared for you, He will demonstrate His power and grant anointing for your life.

As you receive communion pray this prayer:
Father, I receive communion today with focus and gratefulness, acknowledging the death and resurrection power of Jesus.
Thank you for the same spirit that raised Christ from the dead living inside me. Thank you for the table you prepare for me even in the presence of my enemy. I receive your power and anointing at work in my life.

Two

The First Communion

In Genesis 14 enemy kings captured Abram's nephew, Lot. Abram took all the men from his camp and, with divine aid, rescued Lot and everything belonging to him.

Covenant

Verses 18-20 read:

"And Melchizedek, who was both a priest of the Most High God and the king of Salem, brought out to Abram bread and wine.

He spoke over him a special blessing saying, "Blessed is Abram by God Most High, Creator of heaven and earth.

And blessed be God Most High, whose power delivered your enemies into your hands!" TPT

In these verses we find bread and wine first used in a covenantal context.

29

A covenant is different from a promise. Promises are one sided, only one party needs to participate and they can be easily broken without lasting consequence. Covenants are two sided, both parties contribute all they have for the benefit of each other and both parties are bound to it. Two entities become one. They are all in!

Melchizedek was the King of Salem. Salem can be translated as shalom, meaning peace, wholeness, nothing missing or broken. It can also be translated as righteousness.

Abram's active receiving of the bread and the wine entitled him to the shalom and righteousness of the King/Priest. Abram, in turn, gave a tithe of every material thing he possessed. His wealth represented his ability, his effort, his time, even his identity.

The battle Abram had just won isn't described in very much detail. However, it seems to have deeply affected him because he appears to have been experiencing fear a few verses later. Was it fear of retaliation by the kings he had defeated?

Was it concern regarding his mortality or not having an heir? Whatever his fear, it seems God addressed these issues and more in the following verses.

The Reward

Genesis 15:1 tells us:
"Afterwards, the word of Yahweh came to Abram in a vision and said, "Abram, don't yield to fear, for I am your Faithful Shield and your Abundant Reward." TPT
The Amplified Version says, *"Your reward [for obedience] shall be very great."*

The word of God came to Abram. He heard God's voice! God gave him promises, prophecy, direction, wisdom and answers. Peace came to him through God's words. Abram received vision for himself and for his descendants. God's prophetic promise was far beyond what Abram could have imagined on his own.

Deliverance from fear came to him. Whatever Abram had been worried about no longer caused fear after he received the word of Yahweh. Fear is never from God.

Supernatural protection came with God's words, "I am your Faithful Shield." God's shield encircles us. It covers every part of our lives. In the same way the covenant between Abram and Lot required Abram to use his resources to recover what was taken from Lot, our covenant with God ensures God moves on our behalf to restore and make right everything that has been damaged or stolen from us.

"Your reward shall be very great" was God's promise to Abram. Supernatural provision became his in addition to Peace and Righteousness. God wanted to provide for Abram in such a way that everyone would know it was He who provided and blessed.

Our God is a covenant making and covenant keeping God. Communion is a symbol and reminder of God's covenant with us. Just like a covenant is much more than a promise, communion is much more than a ritual.

Matthew 26:26-28 puts it this way:

"As they ate, Jesus took the bread, blessed it, and broke it, and gave it to his disciples. He said to them, "This is my body. Eat it."

Then taking the cup of wine and giving praises to the Father, he entered covenant with them, saying, "This is my blood. Each of you must drink it in fulfillment of the covenant.

For this is the blood that seals the new covenant. It will be poured out for many for the complete forgiveness of sins." TPT

As you receive communion pray this prayer:
Father, today I choose to actively receive the gifts available to me through covenant with you.

I receive your protection, provision, peace and righteousness.

I listen for your voice and release my fear. I trust you for divine protection and provision. By receiving communion, I am recognizing the body and blood of Jesus and applying it to my life.

Three

The Blood of Jesus

In the garden of Eden, when Adam and Eve sinned, God sacrificed an animal on their behalf. Years later, when Noah exited the ark, he sacrificed one of every clean animal to God. Genesis tells us that it was a soothing aroma to God.

In Genesis 9:2-3, God said to Noah:
"And the fear of you and the dread of you shall be on every beast of the earth, on every bird of the air, on all that move on the earth, and on all the fish of the sea. They are given into your hand.

Every moving thing that lives shall be food for you. I have given you all things, even as the green herbs."
In verse 4 God gave the exception: "But you shall not eat flesh with its life, that is, its blood." NKJV

The word translated as life, refers to the life force in human and animal circulatory systems. Blood contains life.

There are certainly health reasons for not consuming animal blood, especially in large quantities. Under the law, blood of animals used for sacrifice was to be sprinkled on the altar. Rather than consuming blood of animals killed for food, it was to be poured on the ground and covered with dirt.

Atonement

God said to the Israelites in Leviticus 17:10-11,14 *"And whatever man of the house of Israel, or of the strangers who dwell among you, who eats any blood, I will set My face against that person who eats blood and will cut him off from among his people.*

For the life of the flesh is in the blood, and I have given it to you upon the altar to make atonement for your souls;

for it is the blood that makes atonement for the soul. NKJV

Blood is meant to atone for sin and to bring life.

Atonement means to make reparations for guilt or wrongdoing. Logically, the one who has sinned should have to make reparations with their own blood. However, in His mercy, God considered the blood of animals sufficient to take the place of our own blood sacrifice.

The word for atonement also means to wipe or erase. The blood of sacrifices was used for cleansing, washing and erasing sin from the Israelites, also from the tabernacle and its contents.

The tabernacle was the structure that housed the altar and the holy place like our body houses our soul and spirit. The altar was where sacrifices were constantly being burned. We can liken the altar to our soul, regularly aligning our mind, will, emotions and reasoning with God's Word. The holy place was where the spirit of God lived. It is where our spirit desires to be - in alignment with His spirit.

Leviticus 16 gives detailed instructions regarding the priest not entering the holy place inside the veil without first atoning for himself, his household, the tabernacle, the altar and the holy place. Of course, the atonement was made with the blood of an animal.

Life

In Acts 15, there was extreme tension and discussion over whether Gentiles needed to be circumcised. Paul, Barnabas and other believers went to Jerusalem to meet with the apostles and settle the matter. It was a convention resulting in an official letter addressing the issues.

They ended the letter with this statement in verses 28 and 29:
"For it pleases the Holy Spirit and us that we not place any unnecessary burden on you, except for the following restrictions: Stay away from anything offered to a pagan idol, from eating what is strangled or with any blood, and from sexual immorality. You will be beautiful believers if you keep your souls from these things, and you

will be true and faithful to our Lord Jesus. May
God bless you! TPT

Circumcision didn't even make the list but abstaining from consuming blood did! It was obviously very important.

In John chapter 6 Jesus was talking with Pharisees in the synagogue. They were aware of the great importance the law put on not consuming blood, so they were shocked to hear Jesus say in verses 53-56:

"Listen to this eternal truth: Unless you eat the body of the Son of Man and drink his blood, you will not have eternal life.

Eternal life comes to the one who eats my body and drinks my blood, and I will raise him up in the last day.

For my body is real food for your spirit, and my blood is real drink.

The one who eats my body and drinks my blood lives in me, and I live in him." TPT

Blood is still required to make reparations for our sin. However, we no longer depend on the blood of animal sacrifices sprinkled on the altar to obtain temporary cleansing. Instead, we receive the blood of Jesus who willingly became the sacrifice for our cleansing.

By receiving communion, we remember and acknowledge His atonement for us. Eating the bread is symbolically eating the body of Jesus, and drinking the juice is symbolically drinking the blood of Jesus. We do it often to remind us there is complete atonement and eternal life in the blood.

As you receive communion pray this prayer:
Father, I am grateful for the blood of Jesus offered willingly for me. I choose to receive eternal life obtained for me through His blood.

Thank you for cleansing every part of who I am, body, soul and spirit by the blood of Jesus. I acknowledge and receive the atonement and life provided for me by the blood of Jesus.

Four

Communion as a Veil

When we hear the word veil, we typically think of a beautiful face covering a bride wears as she walks down the aisle on her wedding day. When I walked down the aisle, the borrowed veil I wore was a bit too large for me. It felt more awkward than pretty.

A bridal veil is meant to only obscure the bride's face; many other veils are made to completely hide what is on the other side.

The Temple

Exodus 26 talks about a veil that hung over the opening between the temple's holy place and most holy place. According to verse 33, the purpose of that veil was to keep people separated from the most holy place where God's presence lived.

God gave detailed instructions for the veil. It was elaborate! Angels were woven into the design with blue, purple, and scarlet thread and fine linen. It hung from 30-foot-tall gold-covered pillars and measured at least fifteen feet wide and four inches thick.

Hebrews 9, verses 7 and 8 read:
"And the high priest was permitted to enter into the Holiest Sanctuary of All only once a year, and he could never enter without first offering sacrificial blood for both his own sins and for the sins of the people.
Now the Holy Spirit uses the symbols of this pattern of worship to reveal that the perfect way of holiness had not yet been unveiled." TPT

The most holy place held the ark of the covenant. On top of the ark sat the mercy seat of God, where God's presence resided. The high priest entered the holy of holies by going behind the veil.

Even when the high priest entered the holy of holies, he carried incense from the altar of incense. Smoke from the incense veiled his view of the ark of the covenant and the mercy seat.

In Hebrews 10:1 we read, *"The old system of living under the law, presented us with only a faint shadow, a crude outline of the reality of the wonderful blessings to come.*
Even with its steady stream of sacrifices offered year after year, there still was nothing that could make our hearts perfect before God." TPT

Many people sincerely desired God's presence but could not yet fully know it because of the enormous barrier, a veil, between them and the fulfillment of their desire. They were dependent on another human carrying incense and the blood of an animal to go beyond the veil for them.

Everything in the law pointed to what had not yet become reality on earth. The veil hanging in the temple was no exception. When God gave Moses instructions for the original veil, He intended to one day trade this symbol for spiritual reality. The day Jesus was crucified was that day.

The Cross

Matthew 27 talks about Jesus' crucifixion in verses 50 and 51.

"Jesus passionately cried out, took his last breath, and gave up his spirit.

At that moment, *the veil in the Holy of Holies was torn in two from the top to the bottom. The earth shook violently, rocks were violently split apart..." TPT (emphasis added)*

At the exact same time Jesus gave up his spirit for our redemption, the veil in the temple tore in two. At that very moment Jesus became for us the veil we go through to approach the Mercy seat of God.

Through his death, Jesus' blood took the place of the veil of separation hanging between us and God's presence; hanging between us and forgiveness; hanging between us and our fellow man. Jesus' blood has become our access to God's presence.

Hebrews 10:19 and 20 says: *"Now we are brothers and sisters in God's family because of the blood of Jesus, and he welcomes us to come into the most holy sanctuary in the heavenly realm- boldly and without hesitation.*
For he has dedicated a new, life-giving way for us to approach God." TPT

Just as the veil was torn in two, Jesus' body was torn open to give us free and fresh access to Him!

Flawless

When my husband looked at me through my veil at our wedding, he did not notice anything awkward or ill-fitting. He did not think about everything I couldn't do or have any doubts about our ability to conquer life together. His gaze through that veil was one of admiration. His heart saw only flawlessness and hope for our future.

Just like a groom looks at his bride through the veil covering her face and only sees perfection, God looks at us through the blood of Jesus and sees only beauty and righteousness. His thoughts

44

about us are filled with good plans for our future.

Read Romans 5:1 *"Our faith in Jesus transfers God's righteousness to us and He now declares us flawless in His eyes. This means we can now enjoy true and lasting peace with God, all because of what our Lord Jesus, the Anointed One, has done for us." TPT*

As you receive communion pray this prayer:
Father, I acknowledge Jesus' blood as the veil that makes a way for me to enter the holiest place, your presence, and receive mercy.

Thank you for receiving my participation in communion as worship to you. I am grateful that when you look at me through the veil of the blood of Jesus, you see beauty and flawlessness.

I receive forgiveness and reconciliation, and confidence to approach you, knowing you only have good plans for me.

Five

Receiving Communion as a Child

If there are children in your life or if you can remember being a child, you know they aren't as concerned with being serious and proper as adults are. At an all you can eat buffet, a potluck or summer camp a child will gorge themselves on things they enjoy most, especially dessert. We need to receive communion like children at a dessert buffet; not embarrassed to gorge ourselves on the bread and cup of communion.

Matthew 19:13-15 reads:

"Then they brought little children to Jesus so that he would lay his hands on them, bless them, and pray for them. But the disciples scolded those who brought the children, saying, "Don't bother him with this now!"

Jesus overheard them and said, "I want little children to come to me, so never interfere with

them when they want to come, for heaven's
kingdom realm is composed of beloved ones like
these!
Listen to this truth: No one will enter the kingdom
realm of heaven unless he becomes like one of
these!" Then, he laid his hands on each of them
and went on his way." TPT

Seek the Leftovers!

Growing up, I took communion in church once a
month. It was a profoundly religious ritual, even
stoic, but not at all relational. I remember how the
people preparing the "elements" protected them
like a secret society. Only certain people were
allowed to prepare it and only an ordained
minister was allowed to preside over the
ceremony. One of the rules I didn't understand
was the requirement to be "at the age of
accountability." How old is that?

I did love grape juice! At our house juice was a
rare treat because we didn't have the money to
buy it. So, I looked forward to communion all
month.

As the pastor's son, I learned to restrain myself during church but immediately after the service I hurried to the kitchen on a quest to see how many little cups were left over. I figured since the ceremony was over the juice was no longer communion. I would consume as many little juice cups as possible before the elderly communion lady came along. Looking back I realize, she probably wondered what happened to all the leftovers.

I believe we are to receive communion just as enthusiastically. Eat and drink as much as you wish. Empty the cup! Gorge yourself on God's goodness. He wants us to come to Him receiving communion with the same enthusiasm, joy and excitement as a child receiving a Christmas or birthday gift.

Seek the Reward!

The Bible says God rewards people who seek Him with their whole heart.

Hebrews 11 verses 1 and 6 reads: *"Now faith brings our hopes into reality and becomes the foundation needed to acquire the things we long for. It is all the evidence needed to acquire the things we long for. It is all the evidence required to prove what is still unseen."*

"Without faith living within us, it would be impossible to please God. For we come to God in faith knowing that he is real and that he rewards the faith of those who passionately seek him." TPT

Children are enthusiastic about anything with a reward attached. While our girls were young we signed them up for every reading program we could find. A school program ended with a free pizza while a bookstore provided an earned candy bar each week with a book at the end. Our local library was their favorite because the prizes grew better each week. At the end of summer, they even met the mayor and received a Certificate of Accomplishment.

The actual prize almost didn't matter; it was a

prize and it was theirs. Knowing each prize would be better than the last one made the excitement continue all summer.

Psalm 103 encourages us to not forget all the benefits God provides us. Forgiveness, healing, redemption and mercy are just the beginning.

Receive Communion with Joy!

Nehemiah 8:10 tells us:
"Then he said to them, "Go your way, eat the fat, drink the sweet, and send portions to those for whom nothing is prepared; for this day is holy to our Lord. Do not sorrow, for the joy of the LORD is your strength." NKJV

In season one of "The Chosen" Jesus builds a relationship with a group of children by making things for them and with them. After all, he was a carpenter. The scenes show possibilities of how the children interacted with Jesus and how their joy grew.

David says in Psalm 16:11 *"In Your presence is fullness of joy." NKJV*

We should prepare for communion with anticipation. Receive communion with excitement in the Lord! Come to Him as a little child full of joy. Jesus loves our laughter and happiness.

Another favorite verse is Romans 15:13.
"May God, the inspiration and fountain of hope, fill you to overflowing with uncontainable joy and perfect peace as you trust in him. May the power of Holy Spirit continually surround your life with his super abundance until you radiate with hope!" TPT

Come with the Faith of a Child!

One of our favorite things about our weekly communion group on zoom is the children who join. We love watching them share their favorite rock or shell, their pets or their created pictures. Almost weekly we see a closeup of one of their eyes. Most of the adults on the call would not

51

wave goodbye at the end of every meeting if it weren't for the children waving enthusiastically at them.

In their eyes we see faith growing. They understand communion should be received with joy and happiness. They watch us pray, laugh, cry and worship together. They see how we apply communion to our daily lives by experiencing with us the highs of families receiving miracles and the sorrow of loved ones passing.

Even these little ones are learning to understand Jesus' payment for our pain, sickness and sin. They recognize how we can experience His peace regardless of circumstances.

Today as you receive communion, do so with enthusiasm and joy knowing your faith in Jesus will be rewarded!

As you receive communion pray this prayer:
Father, I come to you today with abounding joy and wholehearted faith in the sacrifice made for me on the cross.

I receive the forgiveness, healing, redemption and love provided for me through the blood of Jesus. I will not forget the benefits you want to provide for me. By faith I am receiving the body and blood of Jesus.

Six

Communion As Worship

God loves it when we worship Him. We do this in a variety of ways. Singing, clapping, dancing, raising our hands, kneeling, and playing instruments are activities many of us participate in. Giving our money and God given talents are forms of worship as well.

Priests

Hebrews 9, verses 1-3 and 6-8 read:
"Now in the first covenant, there were specific rules for worship, including a sanctuary on earth to worship in.
When you entered the tabernacle, you would first come into the holy chamber, where you would find the lampstand and the bread of his presence on the fellowship table.
Then as you pass through the next curtain, you

would enter the innermost chamber called the holiest sanctuary of all." TPT

"So, with this prescribed pattern of worship, the priests would routinely go in and out of the first chamber to perform their religious duties.
And the high priest was permitted to enter the Holiest sanctuary of all only once a year.
He could never enter without first offering sacrificial blood for both his own sins and for the sins of the people.
Now the Holy Spirit uses the symbolism of this pattern of worship to reveal that the perfect way of holiness had not yet been unveiled." TPT

The things we just read about actually happened and they are symbols for us to learn from. The temple represents our body. The outer Holy Chamber represents our soul and the Holiest sanctuary represents our spirit.

Let's read verse six again.
"So, with this prescribed pattern of worship, the priests would routinely go in and out of the first chamber to perform their religious duties." TPT

The priests routinely went in and out of the first chamber to perform their religious duties. Do we routinely go in and out of God's presence in our minds and emotions to perform our religious duties (attending church, tithing, serving, etc.) without engaging our spirit? Another way to say it is "going through the motions".

I'm sure many of the priests had spent hours as children wondering what it would be like when the day would come for their turn to perform these duties. However, as the years passed it had become routine. What began with awe, wonder and excitement became common religious duty.

Whether heartfelt or duty, God considered it worship. Verse eight says this pattern of worship revealed that the perfect way of holiness had not yet been unveiled.

Today, we no longer need a high priest to go beyond a fabric veil with the blood of an animal sacrifice on our behalf. Instead, we have Jesus as our high priest who has provided His own sacrificial blood. When Jesus died the fabric veil was torn in two. Through Jesus we can enter directly into God's presence.

Eucharist

Communion is a celebration ceremony often called the Eucharist. Eucharist can be defined as gratitude, gratefulness or rejoicing. Eucharist comes from the same Greek word as thanksgiving.

In Psalm 100, verse 4 we read: *"You can pass through his open gates with the password of praise. Come right into his presence (Holy of Holies) with thanksgiving. Come bring your thank offering to him and affectionately bless his beautiful name." TPT*

Leviticus 7 describes the law given by Moses for a thank offering. Verses eleven and twelve teach us that a peace offering became a thank offering when it was offered with unleavened bread mixed with oil. Oil often represents Holy Spirit.

In addition to sacrificial blood, they were to bring unleavened bread.

Verse fifteen tells us:
"The flesh of the sacrifice of his peace offering for thanksgiving will be eaten the same day it is offered. He shall not leave any of it until morning." NKJV

An identical instruction had been given to the Israelites regarding the original Passover meal.

According to Psalm 100:4 you enter God's presence with praise and a thank offering. A thank offering is a symbol of communion or Eucharist that we celebrate today.

We bring worship to Jesus by celebrating communion and by honoring the sacrifice He made on our behalf with thankfulness!

As you receive communion pray this prayer:
Father, I am grateful you provided the sacrifice for my redemption. I am thankful for open access to enter your presence.

I celebrate the symbols of communion you have given me to learn from as I grow closer to you. I repent for times I have let this form of worship become a duty or simply a routine.

I enter your presence with praise for who you are and what you have done. Holy Spirit, I invite you to fill every area of my life as I worship through communion.

Seven

Communion for Healing

Sickness and disease will keep us from God's purpose and destiny for our lives. Temptation to accept sickness and disease as normal can be one of the greatest attacks the enemy uses to harm Christians. When we suffer physically, emotionally or spiritually it can blind us and keep us from all that God is intending for us.

Communion

If you are dealing with sickness or disease, you may already be declaring your healing, wholeness and freedom through prayer. We want to encourage you to add communion to your prayers and declarations.

Many Christians pray and seek God but often overlook communion. Communion is common union with God. Like laying hands on someone or anointing something with oil, receiving communion is a point of contact for our faith and a way of saying "God, I receive all that Jesus died for. I receive all of the healing, all of the freedom, all of the forgiveness."

Just as Jesus did not hold anything back from us, we will not reject or leave anything out of our walk with Him.

Imagine receiving several birthday gifts from your parents but choosing to only keep a few of them, leaving the others unopened. Seemingly, that is what many of us do. It is possible to receive the salvation Jesus offers while leaving other things He defeated on the cross out of our lives.

The Cross

Isaiah 53:4-7 says this:
"Yet he was the one who carried our sicknesses and endured the torment of our sufferings. We viewed him as one who was being punished for

61

something he himself had done, as one who was struck down by God and brought low.

But it was because of our rebellious deeds that he was pierced and because of our sins that he was crushed. He endured the punishment that made us completely whole, and in his wounding, we found our healing.

Like wayward sheep, we have all wandered astray. Each of us has turned from God's paths and chosen or own way; even so, Yahweh laid the guilt of our every sin upon him.

He was oppressed and harshly mistreated; still he humbly submitted, refusing to defend himself. He was led like a gentle lamb to be slaughtered. Like silent sheep before his hearers, he didn't even open his mouth." TPT

Within this passage we can see and understand what Jesus accomplished on the cross was a complete work for our complete healing; physically, emotionally and spiritually! Far more than just a religious tradition, communion is a symbol of everything Jesus died for at Calvary.

By receiving the cup, we are remembering that

Jesus died to deliver us from sin. When we receive the bread, we are remembering that He died to deliver us from physical and spiritual torment. He overcame temptation, addictions, worry, fear, poverty and everything that can destroy our lives, including sickness and disease!

Celebrating communion doesn't need to only be done within the walls of a church. Jesus encouraged us to take it often. Power in unity with other believers is a benefit of receiving communion and a great form of acknowledging our unity and partnership with Jesus. Through communion we are embracing everything He has provided through His death and resurrection.

Every time we take communion we are growing our roots deeper into our faith and strengthening ourselves in the covenant we have with God.

As you receive communion pray this prayer:

Father, thank you for your plan for my healing. Jesus, thank you for your willing sacrifice that provides my healing, freedom and forgiveness.

As I receive communion right where I am, I also receive healing by the stripes of Jesus.

Eight

Overcoming Depression

Have you ever been depressed, oppressed or wanted to give up? It might have felt like the world was against you. We all experience moments where it seems we have gone from the top of the world to the bottom of the pit in a matter of seconds.

Elijah

The same thing happened to Elijah, God's prophet. In the book of 1 Kings, chapter 18, we read the account of Elijah miraculously defeating the 450 prophets of Baal. What a mighty accomplishment! What a powerful display of the power of God working through him!

Immediately after killing the prophets of Baal Elijah told his assistant to look for rain clouds.

After multiple outings to look, a cloud finally appeared. God used Elijah to prophesy the end of the drought.

I imagine that Elijah was on top of the world and felt as if nothing could stop him! He may have felt like he was able to run through anything, jump over anything or fight anyone. Anyone who has ever competed and succeeded knows the jubilation Elijah likely felt in that moment.

Depression

I Kings 19:1- 4 tells us: *"And Ahab told Jezebel all that Elijah had done, also how he had executed all the prophets with the sword.*
Then Jezebel sent a messenger to Elijah, saying, "So let the gods do to me, and more also if I do not make your life as the life of one of them by tomorrow about this time."
And when he saw that, he arose and ran for his life, and went to Beersheba, which belongs to Judah, and left his servant there.
But he himself went a day's journey into the wilderness and came and sat down under a

broom tree." NKJV

Elijah immediately went from the mountain top of emotions to the valley of despair. He prayed to die and said, *"It is enough! Now Lord take my life, for I am no better than my fathers!"*

Oppression or depression will distort your view of reality. When it comes, you can't see anything good. Everything feels sad, gloomy and dark. It can seem completely overwhelming.

Opposite of the veil Jesus tore for us, this veil is one of deception the enemy tries to throw on us. The enemy will speak lies and accusations behind this veil, declaring our faults and capitalizing on our fears.

We could ask "Really, Elijah? No better than your fathers?" Not one story appears in the Bible of the great accomplishments of his fathers. In fact, the Bible doesn't even name his family. It doesn't appear his fathers had accomplished much. We only learn what geographical region Elijah was from.

After reciting everything he could find wrong the loneliness began to sink in. Depression sank in. The enemy had him right where he wanted him.

Most of us have gone through seasons of discouragement, despair or depression. It's during those times people often say things like, "I've had enough. I can't take it anymore. I'm no good. I give up."

The lens of depression clouds your mind and your mood. It can make you not want to get out of bed or ever leave home. Oppressed and depressed people become lonely or isolated because they don't want to be around others.

Elijah, the Lord's prophet, found himself in isolation and despair. He was depressed, sitting in the wilderness under a broom tree. Maybe you feel depressed. Perhaps you don't feel like a champion right now. Maybe you want to curl up in a fetal position and die. Maybe the triumphs of yesterday seem distant and irrelevant!

When Elijah hit his lowest point God showed up. He sent The Angel of the Lord to bring him a heavenly meal.

The Angel

I Kings 19 continues in verses 5-8:
"Then, as he lay and slept under a broom tree, suddenly an angel touched him and said to him, "Arise and eat."

Then he looked, and there by his head was a cake baked on coals and a jar of water. So, he ate and drank and lay down again.

And the angel of the Lord came back the second time, and touched him, and said, "Arise and eat, because the journey is too great for you."

So, he arose, and ate and drank; and he went in the strength of that food forty days and forty nights as far as Horeb, the mountain of God."
NKJV

The journey from the wilderness to Mt. Horeb was long - approximately 260 miles on foot. One meal sustained Elijah for forty days and nights of travel. Wow, what a meal!

"*Get up and eat because the journey is too much for you.*" These words need to sooth our ears. When we become discouraged, downtrodden and depressed we need to eat the bread that came down from heaven.

John 6:32-35 reads
"The truth is," Jesus said, "Moses didn't give you the bread of heaven. It's my Father who offers bread that comes as a dramatic sign from heaven.
The bread of God is the One who came out of heaven to give his life to feed the world."
"Then please, sir, give us this bread every day," *they replied.*
Jesus said to them, "I am the Bread of Life. Come every day to me, and you will never be hungry. Believe in me, and you will never be thirsty." TPT

Communion is not your ordinary food. It is the first superfood!

Communion is necessary because the journey is too much for us on our own.

As you receive communion pray this prayer:
Father, thank you for providing the bread of life for me.

Through the body and blood of Jesus you have given me victory over depression. I come to you ready to receive it.

I believe you will provide everything I need to fulfill the destiny you have planned for me. I choose to believe in you so that my soul will not thirst.

I choose to "get up and eat" because I can't accomplish your plan on my own. Sustain me on every journey, I pray.

Nine

Communion as a Covering

In the garden of Eden Adam and Eve sinned. When they chose to not trust God it set off a chain of events leading to many consequences.

A Robe

We read in Genesis 3:21:
"Yahweh-God made garments from animal skins to clothe Adam and Eve." TPT

The word for clothed in this verse can be translated "robed".

Imagine the shock of seeing death for the first time. The blood-stained robes Adam and Eve now wore would cover their sin and shame. They wore a constant reminder of the sacrifice made on their behalf in His generous act of grace.

Jacob

In Genesis 27 Isaac wanted to bless his son Esau. Rebekah, Isaac's wife, remembered a prophecy telling that their younger son, Jacob, was to receive the blessing from Isaac.

Rebekah took charge. She wasn't going to let go of the word she carried in her heart so she sent Jacob to kill two young goats and bring them to her.

Verses 15,16: *"Then Rebekah picked out the best clothes of her older son Esau and put them on her younger son Jacob.*
She covered Jacob's hands and the soft part of his neck with goatskins." TPT

Rebekah wrapped the goat skins on Jacob's hands and neck. She also put Esau's robe on him. Jacob was nervous to impersonate his brother.

Verses 26 and 27 continue the story: *"Then Isaac said to him, "My son, come near and kiss me. So, he came near and kissed him.*

Isaac recognized the smell of his son's clothes and blessed him, saying, "Ah, the smell of my son is like the smell of a lush field that Yahweh has blessed!" TPT

When Jacob knelt before his father to be blessed, he felt and smelled just like his older brother because of the animal skins and his older brother's robe that he wore. Isaac gave Jacob the blessing of the firstborn.

Grafting a Lamb

When a shepherd has a lamb who is an orphan or will die without intervention and there is a ewe whose lamb has died, the shepherd cannot just put the living lamb into the pen with a surrogate ewe. The ewe will reject it knowing it isn't hers, it doesn't smell right.

Grafting is a process a shepherd can use to trick the healthy ewe into accepting the living lamb as her own. Skin is removed from the dead lamb in such a way that it can be put onto the living lamb. It's like footed pajamas with a hood.

As a result, the ewe can no longer tell that this is not the lamb she gave birth to. It smells and feels and looks like her own lamb. She will nurse it and it will thrive.

At a time when lambs were being raised for temple sacrifices this would have been common practice.

Jesus

Jesus was born in a lambing cave in Bethlehem in the hills surrounding Judah. Bethlehem is a small village where many lambs used in daily temple sacrifices were also born.

Jesus was crucified on Passover to be the sacrifice for our sin and shame, to cover us with His robe of righteousness. He was crucified so that we can know God as our father through the spirit of adoption.

Through Jesus we not only receive righteousness, we also receive a new identity as children of God.

Robes

Throughout history, robes worn as outer garments have been symbols of identity. One's country of origin, social or economic status, occupation or religion have, in specific times and places, been easily identified by a robe.

Joseph's robe of many colors and the "best robe" placed on the prodigal son are additional biblical accounts of a robe serving to identify favor and belonging.

Isaiah 61:10 reads:
"I will greatly rejoice in the LORD, My soul shall be joyful in my God; For He has clothed me with the garments of salvation, He has covered me with the robe of righteousness." NKJV

When we receive Jesus' sacrifice for our salvation, we take on new identity as children of God. Communion is a way to honor and remember God's generous act of grace.

As you receive communion pray this prayer:
Father, as I receive the elements of communion, I remember Jesus' sacrifice to cover my sin and shame. I am covered by the blood of the lamb and wearing a robe of his righteousness.

Thank you for blessing me with belonging, favor and identity as your child

Ten

Giving Thanks in Betrayal

"Those you love most can hurt you worst" is a phrase we have all heard or spoken. Have you experienced it firsthand?

Betrayal

Luke 21:16,18-19 says,
"You can expect betrayal even by your parents, your brothers, your relatives and friends..."

"But don't worry. My grace will never desert you or depart from your life.
And by standing firm with patient endurance, you will find your souls' deliverance." TPT

Jesus also experienced betrayal. Matthew 26 recounts the story well. In verse one Jesus prophesied his coming betrayal to his disciples.

Verses 19-21 tell us: *"The disciples did as Jesus had instructed them, and they prepared the Passover meal.*

When evening came, he took his place at the table and dined with the Twelve.

While they were eating, Jesus spoke up and said, 'One of you is about to betray me'." NKJV

After their Passover meal, one of his trusted disciples, Judas, led soldiers to where Jesus was praying. Judas kissed Jesus' cheek as a sign to show the soldiers who Jesus was. Judas had received a large sum of money in exchange for his betrayal of his leader. Jesus was immediately arrested.

His response was not to get angry. Jesus didn't throw a fit in rage. He didn't get revenge. He didn't get frustrated. He didn't allow his emotions to interfere with God's plan. A lifestyle of total submission to the will of the Father was what Jesus chose instead.

I Corinthians 11:23-25 reads: *"For I received from the Lord that which I also delivered to you:*

that the Lord Jesus on the same night in which He was betrayed took bread;

and when He had given thanks, He broke it and said, "Take, eat; this is My body which is broken for you; do this in remembrance of Me."

"In the same manner, He also took the cup after supper, saying, "This cup is the new covenant in My blood. This do, as often as you drink it, in remembrance of Me." NKJV

On the same night Jesus was betrayed, he took bread and gave thanks! How many of us, when we are betrayed, offer thanks knowing an unjust thing happened?

Forgiveness

Jesus knew He was about to suffer the most horrendous death a man could face for something he didn't do. He knew it had to happen although He didn't deserve it and He didn't want it. His crucifixion was essential for our forgiveness, salvation, healing and purpose in life. He died to give us everything we need to overcome.

Jesus not only gave us communion in this scripture but a lesson of giving thanks even in betrayal. Don't allow betrayal to make you bitter. Don't allow hate or revenge to fill your heart.

Don't allow betrayal to destroy your future. Don't let betrayal disrupt the plan of God for your life. Giving thanks and focusing on our covenant with almighty God is the example Jesus gave us to follow.

Psalm twenty-three lists many benefits of having Jesus as our shepherd. Verse five says, *"You prepare a table before me in the presence of my enemies." NKJV*

Similarly, the Israelites were told to prepare the Passover table for the first time while still slaves in Egypt. They were in the presence of their enemies - but it was a victory table.

When we look back to the Last Supper, we see Jesus sat at the table with the twelve disciples, including Judas. Luke 22:3 says that Satan himself entered Judas. A table had been prepared for Jesus in the presence of His enemy. It was not a table of defeat but of victory.

As you receive communion pray this prayer:
Father, as I receive communion, I give thanks for all you have done for me and all you defeated on my behalf.

I choose to be thankful despite betrayals that have come my way. I choose to forgive. I choose your way of handling situations over my own.

I trust you and I remember that the things the enemy has meant to destroy me You will turn and use to promote me.

Eleven

Communion as Courage

The Israelites had been slaves in Egypt for 430 years. At first glance it seems they were simply carried on the tide in this historical season without any significant role to play. As we look closer, we see they were actually required to be very courageous in partnering with the words God gave to Moses.

Time

We read in Exodus 11:2 -3:
"Speak now in the hearing of the people, and let every man ask from his neighbor and every woman from her neighbor, articles of silver and articles of gold."
And the LORD gave the people favor in the sight of the Egyptians." NKJV

Imagine the terror and intimidation each one must have felt approaching their Egyptian neighbors to ask for their valuables.

Exodus 12, verses 1 and 2 continue:
"Now the LORD spoke to Moses and Aaron in the land of Egypt, saying,
"This month shall be your beginning of months; it shall be the first month of the year to you."
NKJV

There are two words for time; one refers to chronological time, the other is a unique or sudden time for action. It is the difference between a minute and a moment.

Later in Exodus 12 every household was told to choose a perfect lamb and keep it in their home for 4 days. At twilight the beginning of the fourth day they were to kill the lambs.

Maybe the favor they found in Exodus 11 gave them courage to, in tandem, kill the lambs at twilight.

Twilight takes place just after sunset and is the beginning of a new day on the Jewish calendar. God was giving them a divine reset.

They sacrificed several hundred thousand Egyptian symbols of protection not even under the cover of nightfall. If that wasn't enough of a statement, they put its blood on the doorposts and lintels of their houses declaring protection for their families from the coming plague.

Prior to this, when the plagues had not affected them, they had not been required to do anything. This, however, was the courageous beginning of a new era.

Sacrifice

Their dinner that night consisted of fire roasted lamb, unleavened bread and bitter herbs. Unleavened bread spoke prophetically of the haste they would leave in, also to the removal of sin that would become available to us through the sacrifice of the lamb of God.

The bitter herbs they ate spoke to the bitterness of slavery and sin, also to the bitterness of the cup that Jesus would drink as the ultimate sacrifice. (His crucifixion in Luke 22:42 and Mark 14:36)

Eating the lamb with family and neighbors was telling of our need to partake of the body and blood of Jesus who is the perfect lamb sacrificed on our behalf. Communion is unity with Jesus and with other believers.

Dinner was eaten while wearing their shoes and belts and holding onto their staff. They entered the new era prepared for change.

Change

Though freedom from slavery was what every Israelite had been praying for, it may have made them nervous to eat their dinner prepared to go on a journey. This was where they had been born and raised. It was hard but it was familiar, it was what they knew.

Verse 30 says that at midnight there was a great cry in Egypt as every Egyptian household discovered their dead. If the Israelites had slept at all, there is no doubt they were wakened by this terrible cry. Their belongings were gathered and they left as quickly as 600,000 households can leave.

Verse 41 reads:

"And it came to pass at the end of the four hundred and thirty years—on that very same day—it came to pass that all the armies of the LORD went out from the land of Egypt." NKJV

The Israelites were not the only ones leaving Egypt. The angel armies of the Lord left with them. There was no longer any protection left for them in Egypt and they were not alone in the wilderness.

This was not the end of the story but truly the beginning of an unprecedented chapter in time. We are also standing at the beginning of a new chapter in time.

In Matthew 16 Peter acknowledged that Jesus is the Christ, the son of the living God. Jesus responded to Peter *"You are favored and privileged son of Jonah! For you didn't discover this on your own, but my Father in heaven has supernaturally revealed it to you."*

"This truth of who I am will be the bedrock foundation on which I will build my church—my legislative assembly, and the power of death will not be able to overpower it!

I will give you the keys of heaven's kingdom realm to forbid on earth that which is forbidden in heaven, and to release on earth that which is released in heaven." TPT

Now is a critical time for us to live our faith boldly and to use our mouths to agree with heaven to bring the plans of God into the earth.

As you receive communion pray this prayer: Father, I receive Jesus, the perfect lamb you provided to be the sacrifice for my sin.

As I symbolically receive the body of the lamb and unleavened bread, I receive the supernatural courage and boldness you give me to obey your word. I choose to use my words to partner with heaven in this new era.

Twelve

Communion as Vision

On the day Jesus rose from the dead, sometime after Peter had run to the tomb to verify Jesus was not in it, two disciples left Jerusalem walking to the town of Emmaus.

Resurrection

Our story picks up in Luke 24 verse 14:
"They were in the midst of a discussion about all the events of the last few days when Jesus walked up and accompanied them in their journey.
They were unaware that it was Jesus walking alongside them, for God prevented them from recognizing him.
Jesus said to them, "You seem to be in a deep discussion about something. What are you talking about, so sad and gloomy?"
They stopped, and the one named Cleopas answered, "Haven't you heard? Are you the only

one in Jerusalem unaware of the things that have
happened over the last few days?"

Jesus asked, "What things?"

"The things about Jesus, the man from Nazareth,
they replied. "He was a mighty prophet of God
who performed miracles and wonders. His words
were powerful, and he had great favor with God
and the people.
But three days ago, the high priest and the rulers
of the people sentenced him to death and had him
crucified."

verse 21 *"We all hoped He was the one who*
would redeem and rescue Israel." TPT

Sight

While walking on the road the disciples clearly
saw the path to Emmaus. However, they were
focused on their disappointment in Jesus'
crucifixion. It had seemed clear to them that, as
the Messiah, Jesus would overthrow Rome and
restore Israel to prominence.

Cleopas and his companion told Jesus about two women who had gone to the tomb earlier that morning to find it empty. Two angels had told the women that Jesus was alive. The men had gone to the grave to see for themselves if it was empty and to look for Jesus but did not see him.

Like these disciples, we trust what we see with our eyes. Our sight helps us to navigate our world every day. Sight is a great gift! However, our eyesight can be an enemy of our vision.

Dr. Myles Monroe says it this way, "Sight is a function of the eyes; vision is a function of the heart."

Luke 24:28-32 continues the story. *"As they approached the village, Jesus walked on ahead, telling them he was going on to a distant place.*
They urged him to remain there and pleaded, "Stay with us. It will be dark soon. Jesus went with them into the village.
Joining them at the table for supper, He took bread, blessed it, broke it, and gave it to them.
All at once, their eyes were opened, and they

realized it was Jesus!"

"And suddenly, in a flash, Jesus vanished from before their Eyes!

Stunned, they looked at each other and said, "'Why didn't we recognize it was him? Didn't our hearts burn with flames of holy passion while we walked beside him?' He unveiled for us such profound revelation from the Scriptures!" TPT

Initially the men didn't see Jesus because their vision was clouded with disappointment. Just like these disciples, when we look at things only in the natural, our spiritual vision can become clouded. We must trust God and His vision for our lives.

If we are not aware of and sold out to our vision, what we see in the natural will blind us from the vision God has given us.

Cleopas and his friend ran straight back to Jerusalem. By now the disciples believed Jesus was alive. Peter had seen him.

Verse 35:

"Then the two disciples told the others what had happened to them on the road to Emmaus and how Jesus had unveiled himself as he broke bread with them. TPT

Vision

One of the most powerful experiences you can have with God is when you take communion. It's far more than a symbol!

1 Corinthians 10:16 says:

"The cup of blessing which we bless, is it not the communion of the blood of Christ? The bread which we break, is it not the communion of the body of Christ?" TPT

Paul describes communion as the cup of blessing because we are thanking God for what He has done for us through Jesus' precious blood and to release His blessing into our lives through the power of communion.

Holy communion serves as a point of contact between heaven and earth. Everything Jesus paid for on the cross is available to you now!

When the disciples received the broken bread from Jesus they also received a gift more significant than their sight - they received vision.

Vision to recognize Jesus, vision to understand scripture, vision to see their circumstances differently, vision to move forward in life with an eternal perspective, vision to receive all that belonged to them through the crucifixion and resurrection.

As we take communion, I believe we will recognize God in new ways. We will SEE the healing he paid for. We will SEE God's blessing. Everything Jesus already died for and paid for will begin to show up in our lives just as God intended.

You'll have amazing testimonies to share with others in the same way those disciples did on the Road to Emmaus.

In Luke 24:35 we read:

"They began to relate their experiences on the road and how He was recognized by them, in the breaking of the bread." NKJV

Get ready to experience God's power, protection, wisdom, blessing and favor like you never have before through the power of holy communion. It's more than a one-time experience. It is a lifestyle of communion and fellowship with God.

As you receive communion pray this prayer:
Father, I thank you for the gift of sight you have given me. Beyond my sight, I thank you for vision.

As I receive communion, I pray that my eyes of understanding would be open to your plan for me. I receive your wisdom for my circumstances.

Make your word clear to me. I invite your protection and blessing over my life.

Testimony of Healing

I'd like to share with you the testimony of a recent Holy Spirit encounter I had at New Horizon Church during the 2022 Judah Arise Conference.

I believe that as you read this God is going to activate healing and wholeness in you. To those who are contending for healing, we believe your breakthrough is on its way.

Matthew 5:3-4 says this:
"What happiness comes to you when you feel your spiritual poverty! For yours is the realm of heaven's kingdom.
"What delight comes to you when you wait upon the Lord! For you will find what you long for." TPT

These verses have meant a lot to me since this encounter. I realized that I had finally come to the end of my own resources and then there was Jesus.

A lyric from *Prophesy Your Promise* by Bryan and Katie Torwalt says:

"You set a table in the middle of my war
You knew the outcome of it all
When what I faced looked like it would never end
You said, "Watch the giants fall"

When it was released in 2018, this song became an anthem for me.

I suffered with celiac disease for many years. Below is a recap of my journey with this disease and the healing that has occurred.

In 2007 I had an incident on an airplane that would shape our lives for the next decade and a half. During that plane ride I suffered the most severe pain I had ever had.

After we returned home I visited my doctor. He said things like that happen on airplanes with the cabin pressure fluctuations. However, the pain and discomfort became increasingly worse.

I went to numerous doctors, including naturopaths, urologists, and dietitians. Years went by and we had very few answers.

Traveling became a dreaded nightmare. Work became nearly impossible. Some days I could hardly stand up straight.

In 2009 I was diagnosed with Celiac disease. I went on a strict gluten free diet. The condition was so severe we had to change soaps, lotions and shaving cream. We no longer allowed gluten in our home.

Even though that brough some relief, in the spring of 2012 I hit bottom. We decided to sell our home. A place that had thousands of memories would be home no longer. Caring for the home had simply become too much for me to handle.

At 49 years of age, I felt much older than I was. We knew that, without a miracle, I would not be able to continue working.

All our hopes and dreams seemed to be on hold, possibly never to be realized.

Eventually life leveled out and we settled into a life that included pain management and a tightly controlled diet and routine.

Travel remained difficult but was now manageable. With planning I could now speak in front of a crowd for up to an hour without a break. That meant I could train employees and preach at our church occasionally.

I became complicit with my "new normal", accepting that I would live with this disease. We could manage.

February of 2020 the world began to change due to the COVID 19 pandemic. On March 7th we began taking communion nightly with friends. We soon moved the nightly calls to Zoom and invited our church's congregation. Our number of participants increased and we continued nightly communion calls until Passover, May 30th, when our church began in-person services.

We have continued meeting, sharing, praying and receiving communion weekly ever since.

Throughout this time we have taught there is healing through the blood of Jesus. But honestly, I hadn't applied it to my own life because we were managing the celiac with diet and other restrictions.

On January 29, 2022, Pastor Richard Gordon of Bethel Church was ministering at New Horizon Church. He called out that the Lord wanted to heal someone with severe celiac disease.

As I lifted my hand, without anyone touching me, I went down under the power of Holy Spirit.

While I was under the power, I had a vision of a stadium filled with thousands of people. I was on center stage. Behind me was a huge loaf of bread at least 2 stories tall and a cup filled with wine that was equally as large.

During this vision the Lord spoke to me and said, "You cannot teach the communion message with celiac".

While I was under the Spirit, I felt like someone was pulling and stretching the inside of my abdomen. After about an hour I got up feeling like I was under the influence of anesthesia.

Since that Holy Spirit encounter, I have not only eaten gluten, I have also completed a celiac blood test and, of course, it was negative. **No celiac!**

Today I am walking in the complete healing provided to me by Jesus!

~ Joe

Made in the USA
Middletown, DE
22 July 2022

69862557R00057